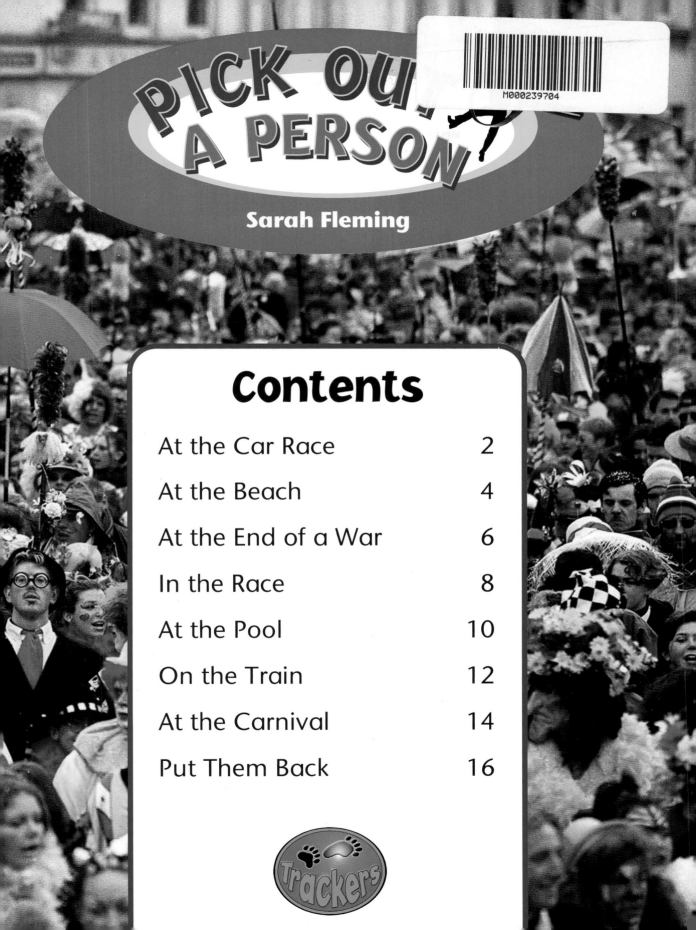

PICK OUT A PERSON

Sarah Fleming

Contents

Trackers

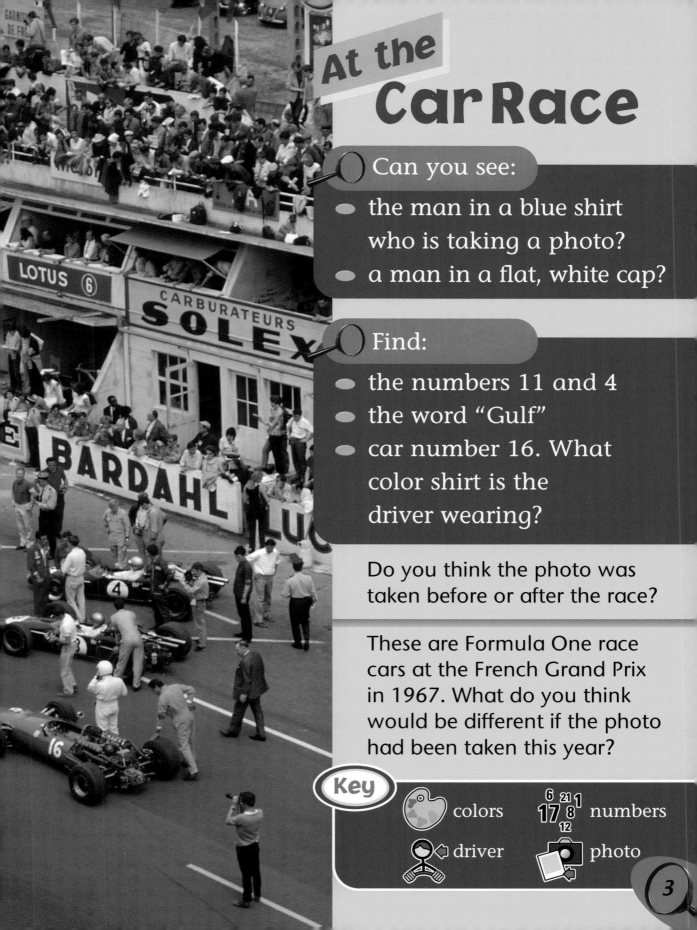

At the Car Race

Can you see:

- the man in a blue shirt who is taking a photo?
- a man in a flat, white cap?

Find:

- the numbers 11 and 4
- the word "Gulf"
- car number 16. What color shirt is the driver wearing?

Do you think the photo was taken before or after the race?

These are Formula One race cars at the French Grand Prix in 1967. What do you think would be different if the photo had been taken this year?

Key

colors   numbers

driver   photo

At the Beach

Can you see:

- the child in the yellow life jacket?
- the child in a purple and blue shirt?
- the man in a pink cap?

Find:

- the boat
- the Jet Ski
- the red flags

Who has just arrived at the beach? Why do you think this?

How many plain, green umbrellas can you count?

Key

boat	Jet Ski
child	life jacket
flag	

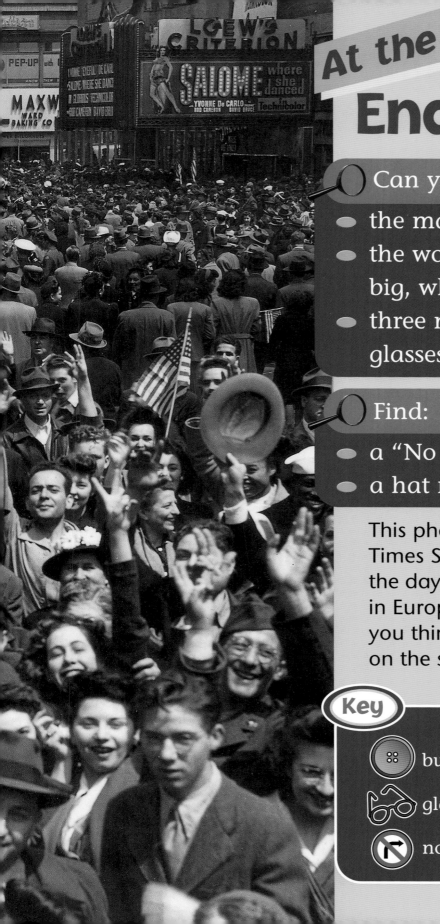

At the End of a War

Can you see:

- the man in sunglasses?
- the woman with two big, white buttons?
- three more men with glasses?

Find:

- a "No Right Turn" sign
- a hat not on a head

This photo was taken in Times Square, New York, on the day World War II ended in Europe in 1945. Why do you think the people are out on the streets?

Key

 button sunglasses

glasses woman

 no right turn

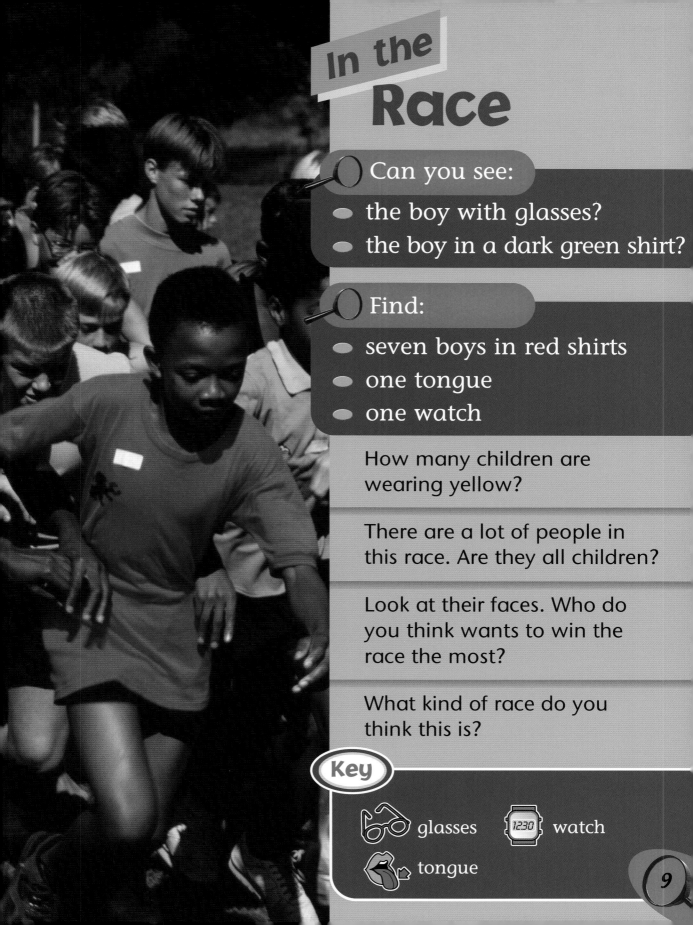

In the Race

Can you see:

- the boy with glasses?
- the boy in a dark green shirt?

Find:

- seven boys in red shirts
- one tongue
- one watch

How many children are wearing yellow?

There are a lot of people in this race. Are they all children?

Look at their faces. Who do you think wants to win the race the most?

What kind of race do you think this is?

Key

glasses   watch

tongue

9

At the Pool

Can you see:

- the woman with a tray?
- the woman catching a ball?
- the child with a fish?

Find:

- ten boats in the pool
- three boats out of the pool
- a foot sticking out of the water

What do you think the woman in the skirt is doing?

This part of the pool is a strange shape. What shape do you think the whole pool might be?

Key

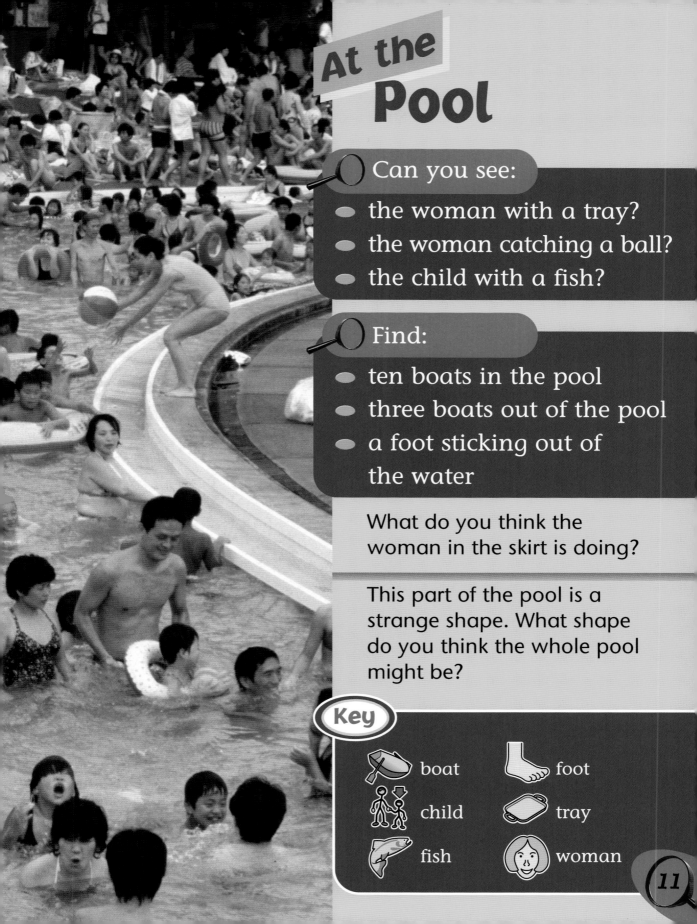

- boat
- foot
- child
- tray
- fish
- woman

11

On the Train

Can you see:

- the man with a green bag?
- the man with a white hat?
- the woman with white hair?

Find:

- steps on the train
- a satellite dish
- a walking stick

Why do you think people are standing on the outside of the train?

Estimate how many people are standing on the outside of the train. Then count them. How close was your estimate?

Key

 hair

 satellite dish

 walking stick

 woman

13

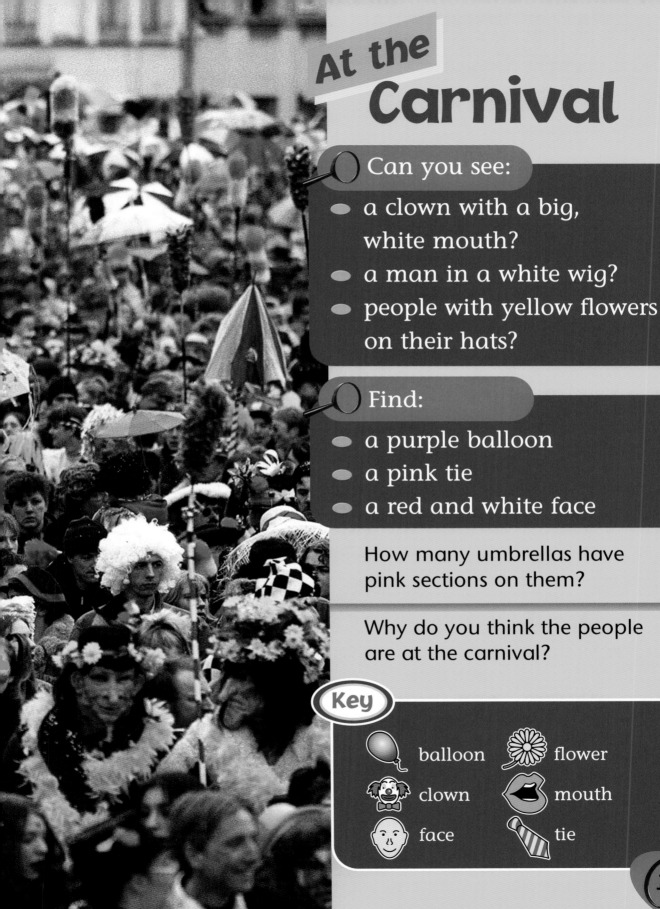

At the Carnival

Can you see:

- a clown with a big, white mouth?
- a man in a white wig?
- people with yellow flowers on their hats?

Find:

- a purple balloon
- a pink tie
- a red and white face

How many umbrellas have pink sections on them?

Why do you think the people are at the carnival?

Key

balloon		flower	
clown		mouth	
face		tie	

Put Them Back

Look at these people. Look back through the book.
How quickly can you find them?

A

B

C

D

E

F

G